PIANO • VOCAL • GUITAR

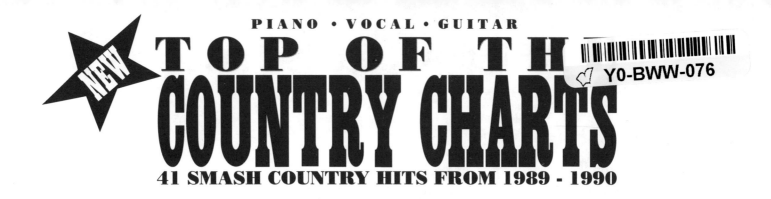

NEW TOP OF THE COUNTRY CHARTS

41 SMASH COUNTRY HITS FROM 1989 - 1990

C O N T E N T S

ISBN 0-7935-0405-8

Hal Leonard Publishing Corporation

7777 West Bluemound Road
P.O. Box 13819 Milwaukee, WI 53213

AFTER ALL THIS TIME

Words and Music by
RODNEY CROWELL

ABOVE AND BEYOND

Words and Music by
HARLAN HOWARD

Well, I'll give you ___ love that's a-

bove ___ and be-yond the call of love, _____ and I'll ___

poor boy's chan - ces for pret-ty girl's__ glan - ces are some - times _____ ver - y
met by chance_ and I knew in a glance_ that I____ found my__ des - ti-

few. Tho' I got no mon - ey if you'll be my hon - ey, here's
ny. And now I____ want to car - ry you off and mar - ry you,

what I'll of - fer you. _ Yes, I'll give you__
if you will a - gree. _

And I'll give you__

buy. _____

ARE YOU EVER GONNA LOVE ME

Words and Music by CHRIS WATERS,
TIM SHAPIRO and HOLLY DUNN

CHAINS

Words and Music by BUD RENEAU
and HAL BYNUM

Bought a tic - ket to Se - at - tle, but I can't get to the plane.
nev - er try to hold me till you see me walk - in' out. ___ I

Ev - ery - time I leave you I keep run - nin' out of chain.
guess you'd rath - er be with me than ev - er be with-out.

My hun - ger for your lov - in' nev - er
You call me back and kiss me and my

DEEPER THAN THE HOLLER

Words and Music by DON SCHLITZ
and PAUL OVERSTREET

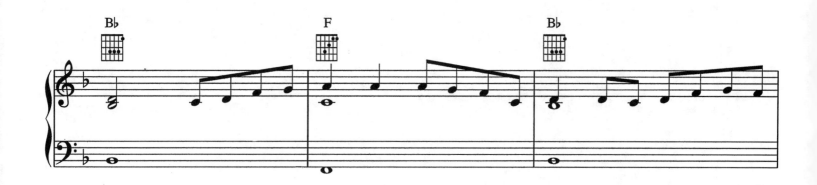

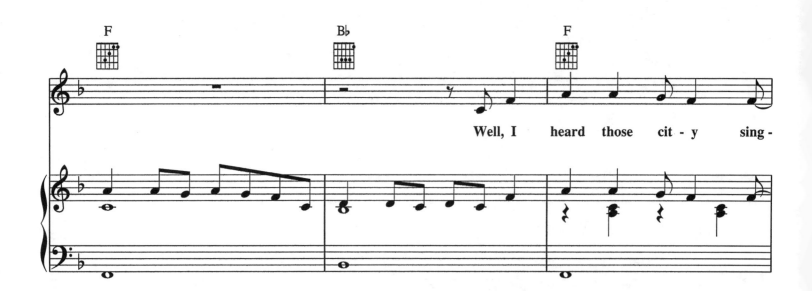

Well, I heard those cit - y sing -

MCA MUSIC PUBLISHING

COME FROM THE HEART

Words and Music by SUSANNA CLARK
and RICHARD LEIGH

When I was a young girl my dad-dy told me a
here is the one thing I keep for-get-ing

les-son he learned it was a long time a-go
when ev-'ry-thing is fall-ing a-part in

if you want to have some-one to hold on to
life as in love I know I need to re-mem-ber

come from the heart _____ if you want it to work _____

To Coda

D.S. al Coda

Now

DON'T YOU EVER GET TIRED
(OF HURTING ME)

Moderately (♪♪ played as 𝅘𝅥³♪)

Words and Music by
HANK COCHRAN

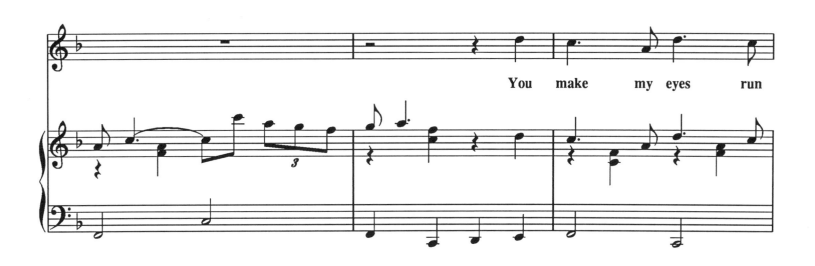

You make my eyes run

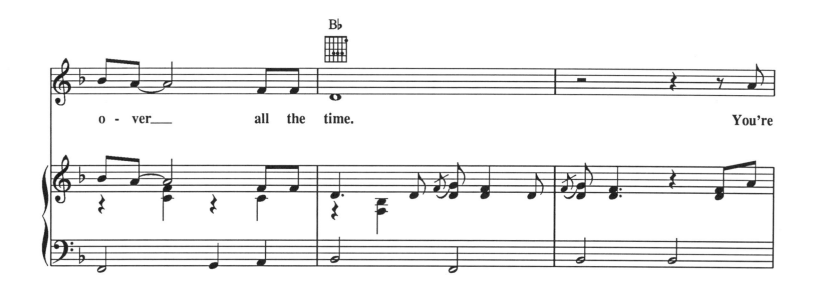

o - ver___ all the time.   You're

You _____ must

Don't you ev - er get tired _____ of hurt - ing

me? _____

(NOW AND THEN THERE'S)
A FOOL SUCH AS I

Words and Music by
BILL TRADER

FRIENDS IN LOW PLACES

Words and Music by DEWAYNE BLACKWELL
and EARL BUD LEE

FEED THIS FIRE

Words and Music by
HUGH PRESTWOOD

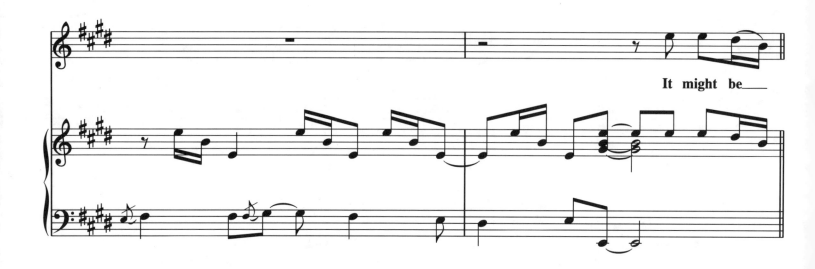

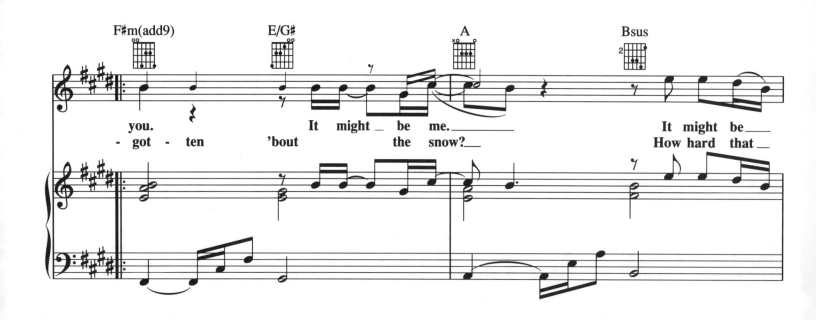

44

HELP ME HOLD ON

Words and Music by TRAVIS TRITT
and PAT TERRY

Ba - by close _ that suit - case you been pack - ing. _ Just sit down _ and talk _ to me _ a while. _ I know you tried to tell _ me what was lack - ing, _ but I guess _

48

HE TALKS TO ME

Words and Music by MIKE REID
and RORY BOURKE

Easy Country Ballad

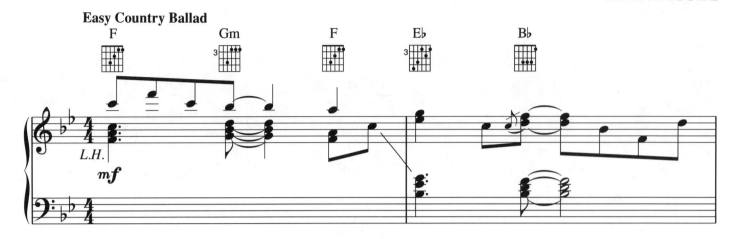

He may not ev-er be ___ a la-
Now you can talk a-bout ___ the fin-

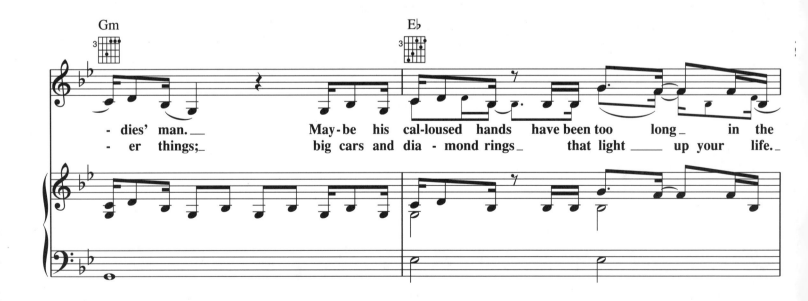

-dies' man. ___ May-be his cal-loused hands have been too long ___ in the
-er things; ___ big cars and dia-mond rings ___ that light ___ up your life.

56

HOLD ME

Words and Music by
K.T. OSLIN

HOUSTON SOLUTION

Words and Music by DON SCHLITZ
and PAUL OVERSTREET

MCA MUSIC PUBLISHING

well. They'll be more_____ than hap-py_____ to put me
way. Your trou-bles_____ will fol-low_____ and

up for_____ a spell. I can
find you some - day._____ There's

hang out_____ or hide out_____ which ev - er_____ I
no use_____ to ar - gue,_____ 'cause he's pro - 'bly

I STILL BELIEVE IN YOU

Words and Music by CHRIS HILLMAN
and STEVE HILL

76

78

Then the moon ___ starts to cry and our

hearts not de - ny - ing the feel - ing we can hold through the night. ___

D.S. al Coda

I still be - lieve ___ in you now ___

some - how. _____ I still be - lieve ___ in you now. __

I MEANT EVERY WORD HE SAID

Words and Music by CURLY PUTMAN,
BUCKY JONES and JOE CHAMBERS

83

I'M GONNA BE SOMEBODY

Words and Music by STEWART HARRIS
and JILL COLUCCI

Moderate Country

Bob - by played his gui - tar on the hard - er side _ of town, _____

where it's hard for a poor boy to find the mon - ey. _

86

yeah. _____

D.S. al Coda

CODA

You know I will, _____ yeah, yeah. I'm gon - na be __ some-bod -

y. _____

One of these days I'm gon - na break _

I'M NO STRANGER TO THE RAIN

Words and Music by SUNNY CURTIS
and ROD HELLARD

good at find-ing shel-ter in a down - pour.

I've been sac-ri-ficed _ by broth-ers, _____

cru-ci-fied by lov-ers, _____ but through it all _____ I with-stood the

pain. I'm no strang-er to __ the rain. When I

94

I'VE COME TO EXPECT IT FROM YOU

Words and Music by DEAN DILLON
and BUDDY CANNON

1. So up - set,
2. A mil - lion times,
3. *Instrumental*
4. I could raise hell,

A nerv - ous wreck. can't be - lieve___ you said___ good - bye. ___
A mil - lion lines _____ and I bought 'em ev - 'ry - one. ___
But what the hell, ___ it would - n't do a bit ___ of good. ___

I'VE CRIED MY LAST TEAR FOR YOU

Words and Music by CHRIS WATERS
and TONY KING

When you left me lone-ly here,__ I
Used to lay a - lone in bed,__

thought that I__ would drown in tears.__ As one was
with my pil - low soak - ing wet.__ All of those

IN A LETTER TO YOU

Words and Music by
DENNIS LINDE

I tore my let-ter up. I could-n't e-ven start to
took the morn-ing sun peek-ing through the trees and the
In a day or two, just you wait and see, you're

tell you what's real-ly here in my heart.__ There's on-ly so much that
dan-de-lion silk tan-gled in the breeze.__ I fold-ed 'em up and I
gon-na get a spe-cial de-liv-er-y.___ You'll know the way I feel. There

109

IT AIN'T NOTHIN'

Words and Music by
TONY HASELDEN

IT'S JUST A MATTER OF TIME

Words and Music by CLYDE OTIS,
BROOK BENTON and BELFORD HENDRICKS

LET ME TELL YOU ABOUT LOVE

Words and Music by BREND MAHER,
CARL PERKINS and PAUL KENNERLY

122

LOVE WITHOUT END, AMEN

Words and Music by
AARON G. BARKER

129

LIVING PROOF

Words and Music by JOHNNY MacRAE
and STEVE CLARK

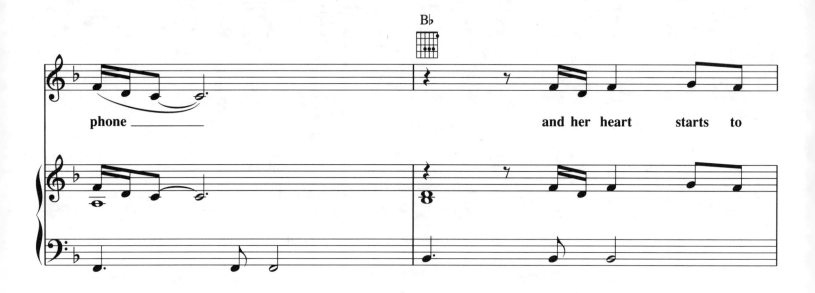

132

136

NEW FOOL AT AN OLD GAME

Words and Music by STEVE BOGARD,
RICK GILES and SHEILA STEPHEN

May - be I'm a ___ game. ___

NEXT TO YOU, NEXT TO ME

Words and Music by ROBERT ELLIS ORRALL
and CURTIS WRIGHT

ON SECOND THOUGHT

Moderately Bright Shuffle

Words and Music by
EDDIE RABBITT

Some - times _ a man _ does
I know _ it's not _ your fault _

Instrumental

things with - out_ half _ think - ing, _ and
that you're_ so_ pret - ty, _____ and

what I saw_ I did _ not un - der - stand. _
that you turn _ the head _ of ev - 'ry man. _ I un - der -

RUNNIN' WITH THE WIND

Words and Music by EDDIE RABBITT
and REED NIELSEN

SHE CAME FROM FORT WORTH

Words and Music by FRED KOLLER
and PAT ALGER

SHE'S CRAZY FOR LEAVIN'

Words and Music by GUY CLARK
and RODNEY CROWELL

out   of ___ con -   trol.

(*Spoken:*) *You know, she's probably*
already to Little Rock.

SONG OF THE SOUTH

Words and Music by
BOB McDILL

Song,   song of the South, __   sweet po - ta - to pie and a

all   picked the cot - ton but we   nev - er got   rich.
we were so   poor____   that we ____ could - n't tell. ____
coun - ty got the farm and they moved   to   town.

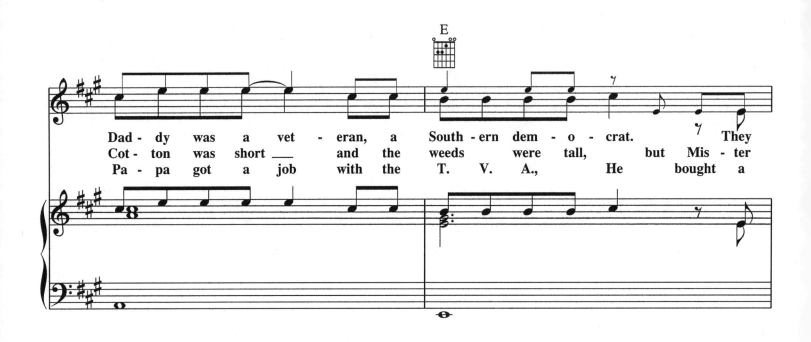

Dad - dy was a vet - eran, a   South - ern dem - o - crat.   They
Cot - ton was short ____ and the weeds   were tall,   but Mis - ter
Pa - pa got a job with the T. V. A.,   He   bought a

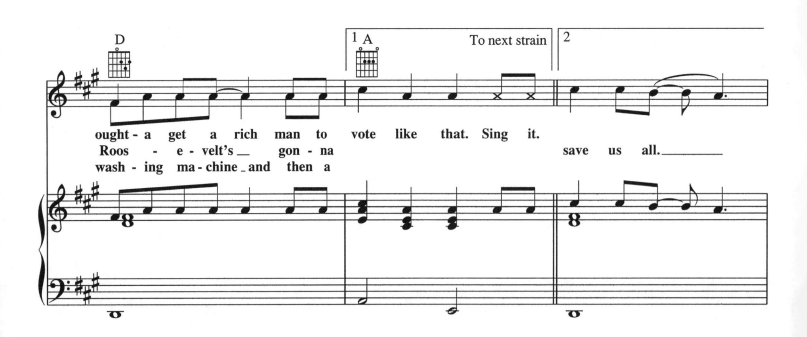

ought - a get a rich man to   vote like that. Sing it.
Roos - e - velt's ____ gon - na   save us all. _____
wash - ing ma - chine _ and   then a

Well back a - gain._____

WHEN YOU SAY NOTHING AT ALL

Words and Music by DON SCHLITZ
and PAUL OVERSTREET

174

you can light up the dark. _____
you   drown out the crowd. _____

Try   as   I   may ___   I   could   nev - er   ex - plain _____
Old Mis - ter Web - ster could nev - er   de - fine _____

what   I   hear ___   when you don't ___   say   a   thing. _____
what's be - ing said ___ be - tween your _____ heart and mine. ___ }

The

Now you say it best ____ when you say noth-ing at all. ____

when you say noth-ing at all. ____

TIMBER I'M FALLING IN LOVE

Words and Music by
KOSTAS

WANTED

Words and Music by CHARLIE CRAIG
and ALAN JACKSON

WHERE'VE YOU BEEN

Words and Music by DON HENRY
and JON VEZNER

190

six-ty years she heard him snore.___ Now they're in hos-

-pi-tal ___ in sep-'rate beds on dif-f'rent floors. ___

D.S. al Coda

CODA

Where have you been?___ I'm just not my-self when you're a-

way. ___ No, I'm just not my-self when you're a-way.

WHO'S LONELY NOW

Moderate Country two beat

Words and Music by KIX BROOKS
and DON COOK

194

WHO YOU GONNA BLAME IT ON THIS TIME

Words and Music by HANK COCHRAN
and VERN GOSDIN

2

Oh, I

G

want to be - lieve you, ___ and I do, _____

D

ev - 'ry time. _____

It's what keeps us to - geth -

202

So who _____ are you gon - na blame it on this time. _____

YOU LIE

Words and Music by AUSTIN ROBERTS,
BOBBY FISCHER and CHARLIE BLACK

Your Favorites in
COUNTRY MUSIC
and more...

#1 COUNTRY SONGS OF THE 80'S
44 Chart-topping country hits, including: American Made • Any Day Now • Could I Have This Dance • Crying My Heart Out Over You • Forever And Ever Amen • Forty Hour Week (For A Livin') • Grandpa (Tell Me 'Bout The Good Old Days) • He Stopped Loving Her Today • I Was In The Stream • My Heroes Have Always Been Cowboys • Smoky Mountain Rain • Why Not Me • You're The Reason God Made Oklahoma.
_____00360715 $10.95

80'S LADIES—TOP HITS FROM COUNTRY WOMEN OF THE 80'S
23 songs by today's female country stars including: Roseanne Cash, Crystal Gayle, The Judds, Reba McEntire, Anne Murray, K.T. Oslin and others. Songs include: I Don't Know Why You Don't Want Me • Lyin' In His Arms Again • Why Not Me • A Sunday Kind Of Love • Could I Have This Dance • Do'Ya • Strong Enough To Bend.
_____00359741 $8.95

THE AWARD-WINNING SONGS OF THE COUNTRY MUSIC ASSOCIATION First Edition
All of the official top five songs nominated for the CMA "Song Of The Year" from 1967 to 1983. 85 selections, featuring: Always On My Mind • Behind Closed Doors • Don't It Make My Brown Eyes Blue • Elvira • The Gambler • I.O.U. • Mammas Don't Let Your Babies Grow Up To Be Cowboys • Swingin' • You're The Reason God Made Oklahoma.
_____00359485 $16.95

AWARD-WINNING SONGS OF THE COUNTRY MUSIC ASSOCIATION Second Edition
An update to the first edition, this songbook features 18 songs nominated for "Song of the Year" by the Country Music Association from 1984 through 1987. Songs include: Islands In The Stream • To All The Girls I've Loved Before • God Bless The U.S.A. • Seven Spanish Angels • Grandpa (Tell Me 'Bout The Good Old Days) • On The Other Hand • All My Ex's Live In Texas • Forever And Ever, Amen.
_____00359486 $8.95

THE NEW ULTIMATE COUNTRY FAKE BOOK
More than 700 of the greatest country hits of all-time. Includes an alphabetical index and an artist index! Includes: Cold, Cold Heart • Crazy • Crying My Heart Out Over You • Daddy Sang Bass • Diggin' Up Bones • God Bless The U.S.A. • Grandpa (Tell Me 'Bout The Good Old Days) • Great Balls Of Fire • Green, Green Grass Of Home • He Stopped Loving Her Today • I.O.U. • I Was Country When Country Wasn't Cool • I Wouldn't Have Missed It For The World • Lucille • Mammas Don't Let Your Babies Grow Up To Be Cowboys • On The Other Hand • Ruby, Don't Take Your Love To Town • Swingin' • Talking In Your Sleep • Through The Years • Whoever's In New England • Why Not Me • You Needed Me • and MORE!
_____00240049 $35.00

THE BEST COUNTRY SONGS EVER
79 all-time country hits, including: Always On My Mind • Could I Have This Dance • God Bless The U.S.A. • Help Me Make It Through The Night • Islands In The Stream • and more.
_____00359135 $14.95
_____00359134
Plastic-comb Bound $17.95

COUNTRY VOLUME 1 —ULTIMATE SERIES
100 top country hits made popular by some of today's biggest recording artists, featuring: Another Sleepless Night • Blessed Are The Believers • The End Of The World • Every Which Way But Loose • Heartbreaker • Honky Tonk Blues • Hopelessly Devoted To You • Lay Down Sally • Let's Do Something Cheap And Superficial • Mountain Love • Ruby, Don't Take Your Love To Town • Stand By Me • Through The Years • Walking The Floor Over You • The Women In Me • Your Cheatin' Heart • more.
_____00361400 Spiral Bound $19.95
_____00361401 Perfect Bound $16.95

COUNTRY VOLUME 2—ULTIMATE SERIES
100 more giant hits: Could I Have This Dance • I.O.U. • Islands In The Stream • Nobody Likes Sad Songs • Any Day Now • Daytime Friends • Flight 309 To Tennessee • Highway 40 Blues • I Always Get Lucky With You • I Wouldn't Have Missed It For The World • I Think I'll Just Stay Here And Drink • Kentucky Rain • Smokey Mountain Rain • Somebody's Gonna Love You • You Put The Beat In My Heart • You're The First Time I've Thought About Leaving • many more.
_____00361402   Spiral Bound $19.95
_____00361403   Perfect Bound $16.95

THE GREAT AMERICAN COUNTRY SONGBOOK
The absolute best collection of top country songs anywhere. 70 titles, featuring: Any Day Now • Could I Have This Dance • Heartbroke • I Was Country When Country Wasn't Cool • I'm Gonna Hire A Wino To Decorate Our Home • It's Hard To Be Humble • Jambalaya • Smokey Mountain Rain • Through The Years • many others.
_____00359947 $12.95

For more information, see your local music dealer, or write to:

HL Hal Leonard Publishing Corporation
P.O. Box 13819 Milwaukee, Wisconsin 53213

Prices subject to change without notice.   Prices may vary outside the U.S.A.
Some products may not be available outside the U.S.A.

COUNTRY STANDARDS
A collection of 51 of country's biggest hits, including: (Hey Won't You Play) Another Somebody Done Somebody Wrong Song • By The Time I Get To Phoenix • Could I Have This Dance • Daddy Sang Bass • Forever And Ever, Amen • Bless The U.S.A. • Green, Green Grass Of Home • Islands In The Stream • King Of The Road • Little Green Apples • Lucille • Mammas Don't Let Your Babies Grow Up To Be Cowboys • Ruby Don't Take Your Love To Town • Stand By Me • Through The Years • Your Cheatin' Heart.
_____00359517 $10.95

COUNTRY MUSIC HALL OF FAME
The Country Music Hall Of Fame Was Founded in 1961 by the Country Music Association (CMA). Each Year, new members are elected—and these books are the first to represent all of its members with photos, biography and music selections related to each individual.

Volume 1
Includes: Fred Rose, Hank Williams, Jimmie Rodgers, Roy Acuff, George D. Hay, PeeWee King, Minnie Pearl and Grandpa Jones. 23 songs, including: Blue Eyes Crying In The Rain • Cold, Cold Heart • Wabash Cannon Ball • Tennesse Waltz.
_____00359510 $8.95

Volume 2
Features: Tex Ritter, Ernest Tubb, Eddy Arnold, Jim Denny, Joseph Lee Frank, Uncle Dave Macon, Jim Reeves and Bill Monroe. Songs include: Jealous Heart • Walking The Floor Over You • Make The World Go Away • Ruby, Don't Take Your Love To Town • Kentucky Waltz • Is It Really Over • many more.
_____00359504 $8.95

Volume 3
Red Foley, Steve Sholes, Bob Wills, Gene Autry, Original Carter Family, Arthur Satherley, Jimmie Davis, and The Orginal Sons Of The Pioneers. 24 songs: Peace In The Valley • Ashes Of Love • San Antonio Rose • Tumbling Tumble Weeds • Born To Lose • Worried Man's Blues • many more.
_____00359508 $8.95

Volume 4
Features: Chet Atkins, Patsy Cline, Owen Bradley, Kitty Wells, Hank Snow, Hubert Long, Connie B. Gay and Lefty Frizzell. Song highlights: Crazy • I'm Sorry • Making Believe • Wings Of A Dove • Saginaw, Michigan • and 16 others.
_____00359509 $7.95

Volume 5
Includes: Merle Travis, Johnny Cash, Grant Turner, Vernon Dalhart, Marty Robbins, Roy Horton, "Little" Jimmie Dickens. 19 selections: Sixteen Tons • Folsom Prison Blues • El Paso • Mockingbird Hill • May The Bird of Paradise.
_____00359512 $7.95

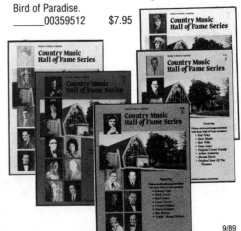

9/89